To Have and To Hold

A Play

Lorraine Forrest-Turner

A SAMUEL FRENCH ACTING EDITION

SAMUELFRENCH-LONDON.CO.UK
SAMUELFRENCH.COM

Copyright © 2004 by Lorraine Forrest-Turner
All Rights Reserved

TO HAVE AND TO HOLD is fully protected under the copyright laws of the British Commonwealth, including Canada, the United States of America, and all other countries of the Copyright Union. All rights, including professional and amateur stage productions, recitation, lecturing, public reading, motion picture, radio broadcasting, television and the rights of translation into foreign languages are strictly reserved.

ISBN 978-0-573-03394-0

www.samuelfrench-london.co.uk

www.samuelfrench.com

FOR AMATEUR PRODUCTION ENQUIRIES

UNITED KINGDOM AND WORLD EXCLUDING NORTH AMERICA

plays@SamuelFrench-London.co.uk

020 7255 4302/01

Each title is subject to availability from Samuel French,
depending upon country of performance.

CAUTION: Professional and amateur producers are hereby warned that *TO HAVE AND TO HOLD* is subject to a licensing fee. Publication of this play does not imply availability for performance. Both amateurs and professionals considering a production are strongly advised to apply to the appropriate agent before starting rehearsals, advertising, or booking a theatre. A licensing fee must be paid whether the title is presented for charity or gain and whether or not admission is charged.

The professional rights in this play are controlled by Samuel French Ltd, 52 Fitzroy Street, London, W1T 5JR.

No one shall make any changes in this title for the purpose of production. No part of this book may be reproduced, stored in a retrieval system, or transmitted in any form, by any means, now known or yet to be invented, including mechanical, electronic, photocopying, recording, videotaping, or otherwise, without the prior written permission of the publisher. No one shall upload this title, or part of this title, to any social media websites.

The right of Lorraine Forrest-Turner to be identified as author of this work has been asserted by her in accordance with Section 77 of the Copyright, Designs and Patents Act 1988

TO HAVE AND TO HOLD

First performed on 21st March 2003 at Norden Farm Centre for the Arts, Maidenhead, with the following cast:

Margaret	Christina Sansom
Susan	Debbie Christie
Lillian	Louise Punter
The voice of George	Andy Barrett

Directed by Lorraine Forrest-Turner

CHARACTERS

Margaret, aged 63 and 33
Susan, her daughter, aged 38 and 8
Lillian, Margaret's sister, aged 58 and 28
Voice of George, Margaret's husband, aged 38

The action takes place in Margaret's home in a small, provincial town "North of Watford"

Time — the present, and thirty years earlier

A licence issued by Samuel French Ltd to perform this play does not include permission to use the Incidental music specified in this copy. Where the place of performance is already licensed by the PERFORMING RIGHT SOCIETY a return of the music used must be made to them. If the place of performance is not so licensed then application should be made to the PERFORMING RIGHT SOCIETY, 29-33 Berners Street, London W1T 4AB.

A separate and additional licence from PHONOGRAPHIC PERFORMANCES LTD, Ganton House, 1 Upper James Street, London W1R 3HG is needed whenever commercial recordings are used.

Also by Lorraine Forrest-Turner published by Samuel French

Seven Stages of an Affair

TO HAVE AND TO HOLD

Scene 1

Margaret's home in a small, provincial town "North of Watford"

The stage is divided into two areas. In the dining-room area there is a door DL *which leads to the hall and a second door* R *leads to the kitchen. A table and four chairs are set* R *of* C. *A duster lies over the back of one of the chairs. A sideboard is set* DR. *A number of condolence cards and a vase of lilies on a cloth are on the sideboard. In the bedroom area a single bed is set* UL. *An old doll lies on the bed*

If required, music plays ("Abide with Me" or similar). The Lights come up on the dining-room area and the music fades. A door is heard opening and closing

Margaret and Susan enter from the hall DL. *Margaret is carrying the post*

Margaret (*looking at the envelopes*) More sympathy cards I expect. (*She places cards on the table and takes off her coat*) I don't know what I'm supposed to do with them all. I can hardly string them up like I do at Christmas, can I?
Susan Mum, you can't stop people sending cards. Besides, Dad would have liked to have known that people are thinking of us just now.
Margaret (*opening and reading the cards*) Sheila and Jim Paterson. We haven't heard from them in years. She stopped sending cards when second-class post went up to nineteen p. (*She opens another*) Bill and Doreen McLeod? Who's Bill and Doreen McLeod? McLeod? We don't know any McLeods.

Susan Didn't Dad used to work with a chap called Bill when he was at Fotherby's? What was his surname?
Margaret Bill McLeod? Could be. From the Midlands. I remember your dad taking the mickey out of his accent when he was round here one Christmas dropping off the turkey. (*She opens the next card*) Only had the one leg.
Susan Bill?
Margaret The turkey.
Susan Dad always preferred breast anyway.
Margaret Hmph. (*She reads the card*) Irene and Tom Hunter. Hmph. She always calls herself Hunter but everyone knows they're not married. Been living in sin for over thirty years. Not that *you'd* disapprove. (*Handing Susan the cards*) See if there's room for them over on the sideboard. Only mind them lilies, there's pollen coming off them all over the place and it's staining that cloth something terrible.

Susan places the cards on the sideboard

Susan They smell gorgeous, don't they?
Margaret Never liked the smell of lilies myself. Always reminds me of dea ... (*She stops herself*)

Margaret exits DL *with her coat*

Susan (*after a pause*) They were all right, weren't they? Down at the funeral directors. I'd always thought they'd be a bit weird but they seemed pretty normal. Really nice, actually.

Margaret enters

I think we made the right choice with the mahogany.
Margaret You said you preferred the oak.
Susan (*trying to keep the peace*) Yes. But I think you were right. Dad would have preferred the mahogany.
Margaret I thought we'd have that haddock for supper. It'll only go off if we don't eat it today.

Scene 1

Susan Mum, you know I'm a vegetarian.
Margaret Well it's OK to eat a bit of fish, isn't it?
Susan No, of course not.
Margaret Well Sylvia Garrett's son eats fish and he's a vegetarian.
Susan Yes, there are some "non-meat" eaters who eat fish but they're not proper vegetarians.
Margaret So what *do* you vegetarians eat?
Susan Obviously everything except meat. And fish.

Susan sees the look on Margaret's face

I'll just have some beans on toast or something. I don't mind really.
Margaret That's not a proper supper. How do you expect to survive if you don't eat a proper supper? I'll do a leek and potato soup. I'll have to give that haddock to Lillian. Which reminds me, she was meant to be dropping in with the sausage meat. We've probably gone and missed her now. If you'd got here when you were supposed to, we'd have been back in time for her.
Susan (*not rising to the bait*) Mum, why don't you go and have a lie down? I'll fix dinner.
Margaret I haven't got time to lie down in the afternoon. Have you seen the state of this place? (*She starts wiping the backs of the chairs with the duster*) I'm going to have to give that living-room a right going over before Thursday and I haven't even started on the sausage rolls.
Susan Mum, nobody's going to be expecting the place to be immaculate. It's a funeral for God's sake. You're supposed to be the bereaved widow not some house-proud maniac who can't stop ——
Margaret (*overlapping*) What do you mean *"supposed to"*? I worshipped your father. I haven't slept a wink the last two ——
Susan I know. That's not what I meant ...
Margaret I can't believe you said that ...
Susan I'm sorry. I was just trying to point out that nobody's expecting you to be cleaning the house from top to bottom at a time like this.

Margaret Let me tell you, my girl, your father, God rest his soul, might be lying in rest down at the Co-op but that is no reason to let standards slip. I have hoovered and dusted this house every day for over thirty years and I'm not about to stop now.
Susan Fine. (*Pause*) Is there anything I can do?
Margaret You can make a start on the soup. There's a couple of leeks at the bottom of the larder. Only mind that sharp knife, it'll have your finger off.

Susan goes off R to the kitchen

Margaret opens the sideboard and takes out an old "Best of Good Housekeeping" cookery book

Susan (*off, from the kitchen.*) Any idea who's coming on Thursday?
Margaret (*flicking through the pages*) Mostly family I should think. Plus a few of your dad's old work-mates and chums from the club. There's bound to be a house full. You know your father, he could walk through the Sahara Desert and meet somebody he knew. Goodness knows where we're going to put them all —

Margaret is interrupted by the sound of the doorbell ringing and the door opening

Lillian (*off L; calling*) Hallo. Only me.

Lillian, Margaret's sister, enters from DL. She has a carrier bag of shopping

Sorry I'm a bit late, they were having trouble with the tills in Sainsbury's and the queues were right back to the ...

Susan enters on hearing Lillian's voice

(*Delighted*) Susan! When did you get up here?

Scene 1

Susan (*giving Lillian a kiss*) Just a few hours ago. I wanted to come up yesterday but I really wasn't in a fit state to drive.
Lillian (*holding her*) No, of course not. Oh, isn't it terrible? Your poor father. And so sudden. Oh, it's just not fair. He looked so well too. We'd just been saying, hadn't we Margaret, how well he looked. I couldn't believe it when the hospital rang.
Susan (*pulling away*) I was still at the theatre when Mum called. I didn't pick up her message until ——
Lillian (*overlapping*) Oh, but it is good to see you, lass. I'm only sorry it's in such terrible circumstances. Still, you're looking well. Doesn't she look well, Margaret? How's life in London?
Susan I've just landed a part in ——
Lillian (*overlapping*) Oh, you poor thing having to drive all the way up here on your own at such a terrible time ... I still can't believe it. This time last week he was weeding and feeding my lawn. Oh, it's been such a shock to all of us. But my sister has been marvellous. You're an example to us all, Margaret. Organized everything herself, she has. I offered to make the sausage rolls for Thursday but no, she wouldn't hear of it. Determined to ——
Margaret Did you get the sausage meat?
Lillian (*taking the meat out of a carrier bag*) Yes, I did but I didn't get it from the butcher. They didn't have any so I went to Sainsbury's ——
Margaret *Sainsbury's?*
Lillian I could pop down to Simpsons' and see if they've got any, if you like.
Margaret (*annoyed*) No. Don't bother, I'm sure this'll be OK. Do you and Brian want a bit of haddock for your tea? I've got some in the fridge but Susan's turned vegetarian.
Susan I've been a vegetarian for years.
Lillian Well, if you don't want it yourself.
Margaret I'll go stick it in a bag.

Margaret exits R *to the kitchen*

Lillian and Susan sit in a daze

Lillian I still can't believe it. He looked so well.
Susan I think we're all in a bit of a daze. I know I haven't taken it in.

Margaret enters with the fish wrapped up in a bag

Lillian Thanks. Brian likes a bit of haddock. (*She puts the fish by her bag*) You look tired, Margaret. Did you manage to get any sleep last night?
Margaret Oh I dozed on and off for a bit but ⎯⎯
Susan Mum, it might be an idea to have a word with your doctor.
Margaret I am not taking tablets. How am I supposed to organize a funeral if I'm doped up on tablets? I do not need tablets thank you very much. I'm not the first widow and I certainly won't be the last.
Susan (*trying to keep the peace*) Would you like a cup of tea, Lillian? I was just about to make one. (*She hesitates*) Mum, how about you?
Margaret What time is it? (*She looks at her watch*) Five past four. Well, it's a bit early but if you're having one yourself.

Susan exits to the kitchen

Margaret dusts furiously. Lillian looks uncomfortable

Lillian (*after long pause*) I'll probably poach that haddock. Nice with an egg on the top.
Margaret (*dusting the legs of the chairs*) I don't know why I bother. The dust's back as quick as you can@shift it.
Lillian (*moving towards the kitchen*) So, how's life in the big city, Susan? Your dad was telling me ... (*She stops herself*) I hear you're in a new play.
Susan (*off*) Yes, we're in rehearsals at the moment but I'm sure they can do without me for a few days.
Lillian What's it about?
Susan (*off*) A lawyer who's being stalked by an ex-client. I play the lawyer.

Scene 1

Lillian Would you believe it, Margaret? My niece a famous actress. Oh we're all right proud of you, aren't we Margaret?

Susan enters

Susan Well, hardly famous but my agent seems to think that ——
Margaret Sylvia Garrett was saying her son's in *Casualty*.
Lillian Oh no, what happened?
Margaret Not *Casualty*. *Casualty*. That programme on the telly.
Lillian Oh, I like *Casualty*. Is he one of the doctors?
Margaret I've no idea. (*Pointedly*) But nice to be on telly though.
Susan (*trying to even the score*) Yes, it's a popular starting point, *Casualty*. And *The Bill*. When you read actors' biogs in theatre programmes you can guarantee half of them have been in *Casualty* or *The Bill*.
Margaret You must be in the other half then.
Susan (*going back to the kitchen*) How do you take your tea, Lillian?

Susan exits to the kitchen

Lillian Oh, just a drop of milk. No sugar.
Margaret (*picking up the cards and dusting the sideboard*) We went for the mahogany in the end.
Lillian Oh nice. He'd have liked that.
Margaret Susan wanted to get the oak but I preferred the dark wood.
Lillian I'm sure it looks lovely.

Margaret appears to be lost in her thoughts. Lillian looks uncomfortable

Lots of cards. (*Pause*) And the flowers smell nice.
Margaret The club sent them round. I've no idea how they even found out. The paper doesn't come out until tonight. Maybe your Brian had a word with somebody.

Lillian I expect so.

Susan returns from the kitchen carrying a tray of teas

(*Relieved*) So when is the play on then, Susan?
Susan (*putting the tray on the table*) It starts a four-week run in Croydon at the end of the month.
Lillian We'll come down and see it, won't we Margaret?
Margaret Not if it's anything like that last one. The only words I understood were the four-lettered ones. I don't know why they don't write decent plays any more. *The Importance of Being Earnest*, that was my favourite.
Susan Oscar Wilde. Wonderfully incisive playwright. Of course he used comedy to illustrate the hypocrisy of the society in which he lived.
Margaret (*to Lillian*) I wanted to go and see the film but George didn't fancy it.
Lillian (*sensing unease*) Nice cup of tea, Susan.
Susan Not that I am trying to defend my previous work but I think you'll find this latest production is more your traditional plot-driven format.
Lillian Not too strong.

Margaret starts to exit to the kitchen

Margaret Right, I need to get on or I'll never get anything done.
Susan Do you want me to make the sausage rolls?
Margaret What would a vegetarian know about sausage rolls?

Margaret exits

Lillian So just up on your own then? Haven't met Mr Right yet?
Susan Well, as a matter of fact, there is someone special but …

Margaret enters and picks up the cookery book

Margaret (*to Lillian*) You'll need to eat that fish tonight, I bought it at the weekend.

Scene 2

Susan (*standing up*) I'd better go and unpack. See you later, Lillian.

Susan kisses her aunt on the cheek and exits DL to the hall

Lillian I'll give you a shout when I'm going.
Margaret (*calling after Susan*) I've left out some clean linen. Make sure you use the top sheet, I don't want to have to be washing duvet covers when you've gone back to London.

The Lights fade on the dining-room area

Margaret and Lillian exit

Scene 2

The bedroom

The Lights come up on the bedroom area

Susan enters from UL carrying an overnight bag. She crosses to the bed, sits down, picks up her old doll and holds it to her

The sound of a radio news broadcast from the early part of the year thirty years ago begins as the Lights change to indicate the past. The news broadcast fades as the sound of George, aged thirty-eight, and Susan, aged eight, are heard. During this scene, the voice of Susan as the child fades and Susan as the adult takes over

George (*voice over*) Close your eyes and hold out your hands. Close them tight. You're still peeking. Now, open your eyes.
Susan (*voice over*) Daddy, you found Rosemary!
George (*voice over*) You left her on the bus this afternoon, you silly thing. Lucky I went down to the station when I did, they were just locking up for the night. Poor Rosemary was all alone with the gloves and umbrellas.

Susan (*voice over*) Rosemary, you bad girl. (*The voice-over fades and live-voice takes over*) I'm going to smack your bottom for running away from Mummy.
George (*voice over*) Oh poor Rosemary. She might have been frightened in the bus station. Go on, give her a cuddle.
Susan Mummy says if you're too soft on them you made a rod for your own bat.
George (*voice over*) Oh, you are a funny thing. Come here and give Daddy a kiss.
Susan I love you, Daddy.
George (*voice over*) I love you, Princess.

The Lights return to the present. Susan hugs the doll to her and begins to cry softly

Susan Oh, Dad ...

Lillian enters from UL

Lillian Susan, I'm just on my way so ... Susan?
Susan (*wiping her eyes*) I'm sorry. I'm OK, I was just ...
Lillian (*going and sitting next to her*) There, there, lass, you don't need to apologize. Good God, I haven't stopped crying myself. You let it out, lass.
Susan Oh, what am I going to do without him?
Lillian (*softly*) What are we all going to do without him?
Susan You're obviously not including my mother in that sentiment. All she seems bothered about is a clean house and sausage rolls!
Lillian Now, now, that's no way to talk. Your mother's devastated by George's death. It's just her way of coping.
Susan I told myself all the way up here that I wouldn't let her get to me but she does it every time. I tell you, Lillian, maybe I didn't come home much before, but with Dad gone I can see me not coming back here at all.
Lillian Now, now, you don't mean that. Susan, I think you should try to be a bit more sympathetic towards your mum.
Susan (*breaking down again*) I didn't even get a chance to talk to him. If only he'd been ill or something ...

Scene 2

Lillian I know, lass. But at least it was merciful for him.
Susan I keep trying to remember what we talked about the last time I saw him. But I can't ... oh I wish I'd known, I wish I'd ——
Lillian There, there, lass, you weren't to know. None of us were.
Susan What was he like, last week when you saw him?
Lillian Oh you know ... Just like he always was. That's what's so hard to take in, isn't it? He was so well. Who'd have thought it, eh?

Pause

Susan Lillian, do you think he was happy? I often wonder if ... You know with the way that Mum always went on at him ...
Lillian (*uncomfortable*) Course he was happy. Why wouldn't he be happy? I know my sister can be a bit harsh but to suggest that your Dad wasn't happy ...
Susan I'm sorry, I just ...
Lillian I know. (*Standing up*) Look, I need to get back and get your Uncle Brian's tea on ...
Susan You're coming back later though, aren't you?
Lillian Well no, I thought you and your mum would want to ——
Susan You have to come back. You can't leave me with her. Please.
Lillian Susan, you and your mum are going to have to ——
Susan Please. Please, just this once.
Lillian Oh, all right. I'll pop back after tea but ——
Susan Thank you. (*She hugs her*)
Lillian (*breaking away*) She's not as tough as she makes out, you know. I'll see you a bit later.

Lillian exits UL

Susan takes a mobile phone from her bag and switches it on. She waits a moment then dials

Susan (*on the telephone*) Hi. How's it going? ... Oh, nothing really, I've just had my phone off for a while and I was wondering if you'd tried to call. ... No, I wasn't expecting you to call, I was just wondering. ... Oh, sorry, what time is it? (*She looks at her watch*)

Oh sorry, I didn't realize. I thought it was much later. I'll let you get back to work. ... I don't know, not until after the funeral, of course. ... Yes, I spoke to Colin earlier, Karen's reading in for me. ... Yeah, I'm OK. ... David ... No, it's OK, forget it. ... No, really, it's just me being silly. I was just — I was just thinking about my dad, that's all ...

Margaret enters

Susan stops and turns

Margaret That sausage meat doesn't look half as good as the stuff I usually get. I don't know why she couldn't have gone to ...
Susan Look, I'll call you tomorrow. ... (*Uncomfortable*) Yeah, me too. Bye. (*She hangs up and puts phone back in her bag*)

Margaret waits for Susan to tell her who was on the phone. Susan says nothing

Margaret I was saying that sausage meat's not as good as the stuff I usually get from the butcher. (*She sniffs the air then crosses in front of the bed*) You need to open a window in here. It's really stuffy. (*She mimes opening a stiff window*) Goodness, this thing's stiff. I'm going to have to get your dad to ... (*She realizes what's she said and stops herself*)
Susan Mum, you are allowed to fall apart, you know. You don't need to soldier on ...
Margaret The soup's on, it'll be ready in about an hour. I've had to put a chicken stock cube in it, it was all I had.
Susan (*exasperated*) Fine.
Margaret (*seeing Susan's bag*) You'll need to hang up your clothes. They're going to look a right state if you leave them lying in that ——

The phone rings

Oh there's that phone again. I'm never going to get on.

Scene 2

Margaret exits

Susan watches her leave. The sound of a radio news broadcast from early summer year thirty years ago is heard, the Lights change to indicate the past. Lillian, aged twenty-eight, enters carrying a children's story book and sits on the bed. Susan, aged eight, gets under the covers. The sound of the news broadcast fades as Lillian's voice, aged twenty-eight, fades in

Lillian (*voice-over*) "... all the better to see you with, said the Wolf. And what big teeth you have Grandma, said Little Red Riding Hood, (*The voice-over fades and the live voice takes over*) All the better to ... gobble you up with!"

Lillian begins "eating" Susan who giggles ecstatically

Mmm ... Yum ... yum ...
Susan Stop it, stop it, Auntie Lillian!
Lillian I'm not Auntie Lillian, I'm the big bad wolf. Grr!
Susan I'll eat you, you big bad wolf!

Lillian tickles Susan. The pair wrestle and giggle together happily

Lillian (*pulling away*) Come on now, sleep time for you. Mummy and Daddy will be back soon and if you're not asleep when they get home, Daddy will smack your bottom.
Susan (*laughing*) He'll smack your bottom too.
Lillian All the more reason for you to be a good girl and go to sleep. Come on.

Lilian pulls the cover up over Susan as the sound of the door opening and closing downstairs is heard

Quick, pretend you're asleep.

The young Susan dives down and hides her face. Lillian stands up

Margaret, aged thirty-three, enters

Margaret (*whispering*) Is she still awake?
Lillian (*whispering*) No. She went off ages ago, I was just checking on her.
Margaret She's not a bad kid really. (*She bends forward to stroke Susan's hair*)
Lillian (*sniffing the air*) Have you been drinking?
Margaret Oh I had a few glasses of champagne.
Lillian Champagne? Where were you drinking champagne?
Margaret At George's office party. They must have had at least ten bottles. I feel a bit funny, actually. (*She kisses Susan's head*) Sleep tight, pet.

Susan starts to giggle. Lillian freezes

Susan I'm not really sleeping! I was just pretending!
Lillian Don't get annoyed at her, Margaret. It was my fault, I was reading her stories and I told her to —
Margaret (*lightly*) Pretending, were you? Well you were pretty convincing. Maybe you'll be an actress one day, after all.
Susan I am going to be an actress. I'm going to be an actress in the London Palladium.
Margaret (*enjoying a rare moment*) The London Palladium indeed! Well won't that be grand.
Lillian I'll er — just pop downstairs and say good-night to George.

Lillian exits

Margaret sits on the bed

Susan Did you have a nice time at the party, Mummy?
Margaret I had a very nice time at the party, Susan.
Susan Did you get a lucky bag when you left?
Margaret (*laughing*) No, silly. Grown-ups don't get lucky bags.
Susan That's not fair.
Margaret No, I suppose it's not.

Susan hugs Margaret. Margaret looks uncomfortable but then relaxes and allows herself to enjoy the contact

Scene 3

Susan I love you, Mummy.

The sound of George and Lillian's laughter rises up from downstairs. Margaret stands up abruptly

Margaret (*distracted*) You'd better get yourself to sleep now or you'll never get up for school in the morning.
Susan I don't have school tomorrow, Mummy. It's Saturday.
Margaret Just go to sleep.

Margaret exits

The young Susan sits alone and disappointed

The Lights fade to Black-out

Scene 3

The dining-room

The Lights come up on Lillian and Margaret sitting at the table. Margaret has various sheets of paper and a note-pad in front of her

Margaret (*to herself*) Oh, I don't know. Which one is the right policy?

Susan enters from R carrying a mug of coffee

Susan Are you sure you don't want a coffee, Lillian?
Lillian Well maybe just a small one then …
Susan (*starting to go back to the kitchen*) Mum? Can I tempt you?
Margaret (*reading the papers*) Now why would I want to be drinking coffee at this time of night? I've enough trouble sleeping as it is.
Susan It's only half seven.

Lillian Er — maybe I best not.
Susan (*coming back again*) OK. (*She sits down*)

Lillian smiles apologetically

Margaret (*looking through the papers*) Oh I can't tell which is which. They've all got the same policy number on them, how am I supposed to know which one's the right one?
Susan I don't think you need worry too much about those. They're just letters. If I remember right, Dad's pension was index linked so they're probably just updates telling you how much the pension was worth at the time.
Margaret I've read this same paragraph three times now. How am I supposed to concentrate with you wittering on.
Susan Sorry.

They sit in silence while Margaret reads the letters. Susan is lost in her thoughts. Lillian looks uncomfortable

Lillian (*quietly*) The haddock was very nice. Brian wanted chips with his but I just had a bit of bread and butter ...

Margaret shoots a glance at Lillian who stops talking immediately

Margaret (*looking up from the papers*) Now. I've arranged to see the vicar at ten tomorrow so ——
Susan (*overlapping*) Yes, you said.
Margaret Are you coming with me?
Susan Yes, of course, why wouldn't I?
Margaret There's no need to bite my head off, I was just asking. Honestly I don't know what it is with you, Susan, but you've hardly said a civil word to me since you got here.
Susan I've hardly said a civil word to you! I was barely through the door when you started on me.
Margaret Well if you'd got here when you said you would we wouldn't have had to rush into town.

Scene 3

Susan There was an accident on the motorway! How many times do I have to tell you?
Lillian Maybe I will have some coffee.
Margaret You could have phoned.
Susan I did phone! You said you couldn't hear me and hung up.
Margaret Well I couldn't. You sounded as if you were shouting at me from the bottom of a well.
Susan (*trying not to get angry*) I was on hands-free.
Margaret You could have stopped at a service station and used a proper phone.
Susan Oh yes, they leave a special lane clear in a six mile tailback so people can get off the motorway and phone their mothers!
Lillian I'll just go help myself, shall I?
Margaret This is all the thanks you get for doing your best and making a nice home for your family.
Susan Oh for goodness sake.
Margaret You're obviously ashamed of the place. You haven't brought a boyfriend home in years.
Susan I haven't lived here in years!
Margaret We never know what you're up to from one week to the next.
Lillian I could make tea, Margaret, if you prefer.
Margaret You're always swanning off somewhere with your fancy friends. It's always me who has to pick up the phone. It's OK for you, isn't it, living it up down in London. Hmph. I wish I could have gone to drama school but no I had to stay home and look after your Aunt Lillian.
Lillian I wouldn't have minded staying on …
Margaret We were lucky they were able to see us down at the Co-op. We were supposed to have been there at twelve. I think you're more interested in that play of yours than you are in your father's funeral.
Susan (*biting her tongue*) I've said I'm sorry. I thought I'd left in plenty of time. Obviously I was wrong.

The phone rings in the hall

Margaret Oh not that thing again. It hasn't stopped all day.
Lillian Do you want me to get it?
Margaret Yes. Only tell them I'm having a lie down and to phone back tomorrow.

Lillian exits DL *to the hall*

Susan (*softening*) Mum, do you think we could just try to ——
Margaret I was thinking of having "All Things Bright and Beautiful" and "The Lord's My Shepherd" at the church. What do you think?
Susan I think we should talk.
Margaret And I was going to ask your Uncle Dennis to do the reading.
Susan Mum, why won't you ——
Margaret The cars will be coming here at half nine so we need to make sure we're ——

Lillian enters

Lillian I'm sorry, it's Dennis, he wants to know if he's doing the reading on Thursday.
Margaret Well I'm not sure. I was half-thinking of asking Tom Arnold.
Lillian He seems pretty keen to talk to you.
Margaret (*harshly*) Just tell him I need to think about it. (*She pauses*) I'll give him a phone tomorrow.
Lillian Couldn't you just ...

Lillian sees Margaret's expression

  I'll tell him.

Lillian exits

Susan What are you going to hide behind after Thursday?
Margaret Such a shame he never saw a grandchild.

Scene 3

Susan Oh good one. Turn it back on me again.
Margaret He'd have liked a grandson. Could have taken him shooting with him at the weekends.
Susan Why won't you talk to me?
Margaret But I suppose if you spend your time mixing with them — actors — you're hardly going to find yourself a proper man ... Even if they start out normal, they end up that way. Look what they did to Rock Hudson.
Susan For God's sake. My father is dead. Your husband is dead and all you seem to be ——
Margaret (*getting up*) Oh I'd better go and talk to Dennis, Lillian will only end up saying something she shouldn't.

Margaret exits DL

Susan (*shouting after her*) Things don't go away just because you refuse to talk about them you know.

The sound of a radio news broadcast from the late part of the year thirty years ago fades in. The Lights change

Susan, aged eight, is standing at the end of her bed, holding the doll. She leans forward as if trying to hear voices in another room. The radio broadcast fades out as Margaret's voice, aged thirty-three, fades in

Margaret (*voice over*) It's not like in the olden days, they're all done in hospitals now.
Lillian (*voice over*) It'd be like murdering my own baby.

Lighting to indicate the past comes up on Margaret, aged thirty-three, and Lillian, aged twenty-eight, DL

Margaret (*the live-voice takes over*) Well it's a pity you hadn't thought of that before you ... Before you got yourself into this mess.

Lillian Ssh. Keep your voice down. Susan's upstairs.
Margaret Don't you tell me to keep my voice down in my own house!

The Lights fade on Susan but remain on Margaret and Lillian

Lillian I'm sorry. I don't know what I'm saying, but if Susan finds out ...
Margaret Susan will never find out! No-one will ever find out.
Lillian Not even ——
Margaret No! If you say one word to anyone about this you will never step foot inside this house again. Do you hear me? Do you hear me?
Lillian I won't say anything.
Margaret We'll go see the doctor in the morning.
Lillian I could marry Brian Henderson. He's always asking me. He wouldn't need to know that the baby wasn't ——
Margaret We'll go see the doctor in the morning.
Lillian If you think that's best.

The Lights change back to the present

Margaret exits

Susan returns to the table and Lillian, aged fifty-eight, crosses to Susan

Lillian Dennis seemed ever so upset. I'm glad Margaret's having a word with him. He says he's got it all worked out. Jeremiah. Chapter Three. Verses Sixteen to ... Or was it Matthew?
Susan (*in a dream*) I'm having an affair with a married man.
Lillian (*embarrassed*) Oh, that's nice.
Susan He has two young children so he can't leave his wife.
Lillian Er — no ... You wouldn't want him to do that.
Susan I had an abortion last year. He thought it was for the best.
Lillian Susan, I don't think you should be telling me this.

Scene 3   21

Susan You'd have thought I was going to have a wisdom tooth out.
Lillian Er ... (*She looks at her watch*) Is that the time? I'd better be making tracks. You know what your Uncle Brian is like.
Susan Nobody makes you feel guilty any more.
Lillian (*hovering by the door*) Well, I'll see you on Thursday then.
Susan I wanted them to make me feel guilty.

Margaret enters from DL

Margaret He's going to do Matthew. I don't know what I'm going to say to Tom. He always does the reading at Easter. (*To Lillian*) You off then?
Lillian I er — thought I'd get going before it got too dark.
Susan (*deliberately*) Mum was saying it was a shame that Dad would never see his grandchildren.
Lillian Er ... No, he'd have liked grandchildren.
Margaret Are you and Brian coming here first on Thursday or going straight to the crematorium?
Lillian I er — hadn't really thought ... Well we could come here first if you wanted ...
Susan No grandchildren. No sons. No nieces. No nephews. Just me. One offspring per four adults. Well five if you count me too. Not really doing our bit for procreation, are we? Didn't you and Brian want a family, Lillian?
Margaret You don't go asking people personal questions like that. I don't know what's got into you, honestly I don't. But you've been in a funny mood ever since you got here.
Susan Funny mood! My father has just died, what kind of mood am I supposed to be in! It may surprise you to learn that there's more to bereavement than polishing the Lladros and making fucking sausage rolls!
Margaret May I remind you young lady that you are not on stage now. So you can keep your foul language and your melodramatics out of here.
Susan Oh isn't that just typical? Why is it that whenever anyone shows any emotion in this house you ignore or belittle it?

Margaret You spend too much of your time with Yanks, that's your trouble. You'll be telling us you're in therapy next.
Susan And what if I am? Whose fault would that be?
Margaret (*walking away*) I'm making myself a cup of tea, would you like one Lillian?
Lillian Well I really ought to be ⎯⎯
Susan (*to Margaret*) Don't you dare. Stop avoiding the issue. Stay here and talk to me!

Margaret starts to speak but stops herself

Stop hiding behind this hard-done-by, pseudo working-class, cleanliness-is-next-to-Godliness façade.
Margaret (*overlapping*) Don't you tell me what to do, young lady. I don't know who you think you are talking to ⎯⎯
Susan (*overlapping*) God, no wonder Dad found any excuse to get out of this house. Every time he walked in the front door you had a go at him for something. Why hadn't he worn his coat? Why didn't he phone if he was going to be late?
Margaret (*overlapping*) I don't know where you get this from ⎯⎯
Susan (*overlapping*) When was he going to put up that shelf in the bathroom? Had he seen how long the grass had got? Did he know that that shirt he'd put in the washing was barely dirty? On and on and on and on.
Margaret Maybe you should have an early night.
Susan What the hell is wrong with you? Don't you have any feelings at all? What do I have to do to get through to you?
Margaret (*overlapping*) I'm not standing for this ⎯⎯
Susan You want to know why I never bring a boyfriend back here? You want to know why I'm not married and supplying you with a brood of happy grandchildren?
Margaret (*overlapping*) I couldn't care less about your love-life ⎯⎯
Susan (*overlapping*) I'd like to say it's because I never learned to love — because if I did learn to love, Mother, it certainly wasn't from you. No, the reason I'm not married is because the man I love is. Yes, Mother, I am having an affair with a married man. I sleep with another woman's husband. I am a harlot. Happy now?

Scene 3   23

Margaret You youngsters think you invented sex. Well, people had affairs in my day too, you know. Only we didn't go around telling everyone. We knew how to be discreet.
Susan You mean you knew how to emotionally blackmail your sister into having an abortion because you couldn't bear the scandal! Is that what you call discretion, Mother!
Lillian (*by the kitchen exit*) I'll see you Thursday.
Susan Lillian. I'm sorry — I'm sorry. That was really stupid of me. I'm so sorry, I didn't mean ...
Lillian I don't know what you're talking about ...
Susan It's none of my business. I'm sorry. You're the last person in the world I'd want to upset.
Lillian I'm — I'm not upset. Why should I be upset? I don't know what you're talking about.
Susan It's OK. I know about the baby ——
Margaret (*overlapping*) Lillian, you'd better not leave it too late to ——
Susan (*overlapping*) We don't have to go on pretending. We don't have to lie for her any more.
Lillian (*overlapping*) I don't know what you mean.
Margaret Susan, I don't know what you think you know but we're having no more of it, do you hear?
Susan What are you going to do? Send me to my room without supper? You think you can control everyone. You think that if you don't talk about something, it never existed. Are you going to stand there and tell me to my face that you didn't force Lillian into having an abortion? Are you?
Margaret The subject is closed.
Susan (*to Lillian*) Why do you let her do this to you? Why don't you tell her how much you despise her? Why don't you tell her she has no right to interfere in your life? Tell her! Tell her!
Lillian Because — because ... (*She breaks down*)
Susan Tell her the truth! Tell her!
Margaret Get to your room! Get out of here! Get out!
Lillian I'm sorry, Margaret, I'm sorry, I'm sorry, I'm sorry.
Susan Look what you've done to her. Look what you've turned her into!

Lillian (*screaming*) NO!! You're wrong. You're wrong. You're so wrong.
Margaret Lillian! Don't say another word.
Lillian It was your father's baby! It was George's baby! I murdered George's baby ... Oh God, God, no ... I'm sorry. I'm sorry. Oh, George, George ...

No-one speaks. Margaret goes to Lillian to comfort her

Susan (*stunned*) Dad and Lillian? Lillian was having Dad's baby?
Margaret Happy now?
Susan Oh God. All these years. I don't believe it ... Dad and Lillian. (*To Margaret*) Your own sister?
Lillian (*through tears*) You weren't supposed to find out ... Nobody was supposed to find —
Susan I can't believe that you all just carried on as if everything was normal. All those birthdays and Christmases and holidays and weekends ... Everyone together. (*To Lillian*) You were having his baby? Dad's baby? (*Suddenly realizing the enormity of things*) My God, it would have been my brother or sis ...
Lillian Oh don't, don't make it worse — please ...
Susan (*to Margaret*) How could you just go on as if nothing had happened? Why didn't anyone tell me? Did he love her? Was he going to leave us?

Margaret bites her tongue. Lillian is terrified to speak

(*To Lillian*) Did you love him? How long did it go on? Did he know about the baby? My God, how could you go on seeing him? Seeing Mum? Seeing me?

Susan is infuriated by Margaret's seemingly cold response

(*To Margaret*) Talk to me! God! I don't know why I'm so surprised. I mean you can hardly blame him, can you? He wasn't exactly showered with love by his wife, was he? I mean, men do want more from marriage than three hot meals a day and a spotless

Scene 3　　　　　　　　　　　　　　　　　　　　　　　25

bathroom, you know! What's that old saying, "if he's not getting it at home he's bound to" ——

Margaret (*finally exploding*) What do you know about my life! What do you know about anything! Oh, it had to be my fault, hadn't it? Couldn't possibly be your precious father's! Not Mr Perfect! Is that what your man tells you, eh? That he's not "getting it at home". That she's always too tired running a house, looking after his kids, washing and ironing his shirts, cooking his meals, cleaning up his filthy mess. (*Releasing forty years of frustration*) You stand there and you tell me what men want from marriage! What about women? What about me? What did I ever get from him? What did I ever get from the pair of you? (*Turning on Lillian*) What did I ever get from anyone? (*Turning back to Susan*) I went from looking after my mother to looking after Lillian to looking after my husband to looking after you. And what thanks did I get? (*Furiously*) If all I ever did was cook and clean and keep a nice house, it was because it was all I ever could do!

Margaret flings her arm out and deliberately knocks over all the cards and flowers on the sideboard

(*Softly*) Forty years I lived with him and in all that time I never made him as happy as she did in one night.

Lillian weeps. Margaret tries desperately to hold back the tears

Susan Oh Mum, Mum, I'm sorry, I'm sorry, I'm sorry ...

Susan dashes to Margaret and throws herself into her arms. Margaret finally collapses and they weep together

Margaret (*pulling away gently*) Go to your Aunt Lillian, pet. She needs you.

Susan looks up in disbelief

Go to her.

Susan goes to Lillian who breaks down and sobs in Susan's arms

(*Mustering all the dignity she can manage*) I'm going to put the kettle on. Would anyone like a cup of tea?
Lillian Well — if you're making one yourself.
Susan Thank you, that would be lovely.

Margaret walks towards the kitchen and pauses

Margaret Maybe you could do the reading on Thursday, Susan? Put that trained voice of yours to good use for a change, eh?
Susan I'd be honoured.
Margaret (*nodding her head and smiling at her daughter*) Good.

Margaret exits to the kitchen

Lillian smiles and takes a handkerchief from her bag. Susan picks up the cards and flowers as the Lights fade to Black-out

CURTAIN

FURNITURE AND PROPERTY LIST

Scene 1

On stage: DINING-ROOM AREA
Dining-table
Four chairs. *Over back of one*: duster
Sideboard. *On it*: vase of lilies on a cloth, condolence cards.
   In cupboard: old copy of *The Best of Good Housekeeping*

BEDROOM AREA
Bed. *On it*: bedclothes, old doll

Off stage: Three condolence cards in sealed envelopes (**Margaret**)
Shopping, including sausage meat, in a carrier bag (**Lillian**)
Fish in a bag (**Margaret**)
Tray of tea for three (**Susan**)

Personal: **Margaret**: wrist-watch (worn throughout)
Susan: wrist-watch (worn throughout)
Lillian: wrist-watch (worn throughout)

Scene 2

Strike: Tray of tea and shopping from dining-room area

Off stage: Overnight bag containing a mobile phone (**Susan**)
Children's story book (**Margaret**)

Scene 3

Set: Sheets of paper, note-pad, pen on dining-table
Lillian's handbag containing handkerchief in dining-room area

Off stage: Mug of coffee (**Susan**)

LIGHTING PLOT

Property fittings required: nil
2 interiors, the same scene throughout

SCENE 1

To open: General lighting on dining-room area

Cue 1	**Margaret**: " ... back to London."	(Page 9)
	Fade to black-out	

SCENE 2

To open: General lighting on bedroom area

Cue 2   **Susan** holds her old doll   (Page 9)
        Change to indicate the past

Cue 3   **George** (voice over): "I love you, Princess."   (Page 10)
        Revert to general lighting

Cue 4   **Susan** watches **Margaret** leave   (Page 13)
        Change to indicate the past

Cue 5   The young **Susan** sits alone   (Page 15)
        Fade to black-out

SCENE 3

To open: General lighting on dining-room area

Cue 6   **Susan**: " ... to talk about them you know."   (Page 19)
        Crossfade to bedroom area to indicate the past

Cue 7	**Lillian** (voice over): " … my own baby." *Bring up lighting* DL *to indicate the past*	(Page 19)
Cue 8	**Margaret**: " … in my own house." *Fade on bedroom area*	(Page 20)
Cue 9	**Lillian**: "If you think that's best." *Revert to general lighting on dining-room area*	(Page 20)
Cue 10	**Susan** picks up the cards and flowers *Fade to black-out*	(Page 26)

EFFECTS PLOT

Cue 1 Beofre Lights up (Page 1)
Music plays; fade when ready, front door opening and closing

Cue 2 **Margaret**: " ... to put them all —— " (Page 4)
Doorbell; front door opening and closing

Cue 3 **Susan** holds her old doll (Page 9)
Radio news broadcast from the early part of the year, thirty years ago, cross fading into voice over as script pages 9-10

Cue 4 **Margaret**: " ... leave them lying in that —— " (Page 12)
Phone rings in the hall

Cue 5 **Susan** watches **Margaret** leave (Page 13)
Radio news broadcast from early summer thirty years ago, cross fading into voice over as script page 13

Cue 6 **Lillian** pulls the cover up over **Susan** (Page 13)
Front door opening and closing

Cue 7 **Susan**: "I love you, Mummy." (Page 15)
*Sound of **George**'s and **Lillian**'s laughter from downstairs*

Cue 8 **Susan**: "Obviously I was wrong." (Page 17)
Phone rings in the hall

Cue 9 **Susan**: " ... to talk about them you know." (Page 19)
Radio news broadcast from thirty years earlier fades in; crossfade to voice over as script page 19

www.ingramcontent.com/pod-product-compliance
Lightning Source LLC
Chambersburg PA
CBHW070454050426
42450CB00012B/3272